CORRUPTED BY MY OWN

The Tragic Tale of a Rogue Roommate

Victoria Jeffery

Disclaimer

The material in this book is meant to be reliable and factual on the topics it covers. Neither the publisher nor the author is providing psychological or other professional services via its sale. If professional advice or help is required, a qualified practitioner should be contacted.

Table of Contents

Disclaimer

Introduction

Chapter One

The Beginning

Chapter Two

The Descent

Chapter Three

The Consequences

Chapter Four

The Turning Point

Chapter Five

The Lessons

Introduction

When I first met my roommate, I thought I had hit the jackpot. She was friendly, and outgoing, and seemed like the perfect person to share an apartment with. But as time went on, I began to realize that there was more to her than met the eye.

As I got to know her better, I discovered that she was corrupt and manipulative; willing to do whatever it took to get what she wanted. She would lie, cheat, and steal to get ahead, and she didn't care who she hurt in the process.

At first, I tried to ignore her behavior and hoped that things would get better on their own. But as the situation escalated, I knew that I had to do something. I couldn't continue living with a corrupt roommate, and I had to find a way to escape her grasp.

This book is the story of my journey to break free from a corrupt roommate and take control of my own life. It's a tale of self-discovery, resilience, and the power of standing up for what you believe in. If you've ever felt trapped in a toxic situation, this book is for you. So, buckle up and join me on a thrilling and inspiring journey of survival and self-discovery.

Chapter One

The Beginning

It was a typical Monday morning when I first met my new roommate, Sarah. We had both just moved into our college dorm room, excited for the new adventures that lay ahead. I had been assigned to live with Sarah through the housing office, and I had no idea what to expect.

As we unpacked our things and got settled in, I couldn't help but feel nervous. I had always been a bit of an introvert, and the thought of living with someone I didn't know was intimidating. But Sarah immediately put me at ease with her friendly and outgoing personality. She was chatty and full of energy, and she seemed genuinely excited to be starting college.

At first, Sarah seemed like the perfect roommate. She was always up for a good time and seemed to know everyone on campus. We quickly fell into a routine of studying together in the library and hanging out with our mutual friends on the weekends.

But as the weeks went by, I started to notice some strange behavior from Sarah. She would often come home late at night, stumbling and slurring her words. I noticed that she had developed a sudden interest in partying and drinking, and she would often disappear for days at a time without any explanation.

Despite my concerns, I didn't want to confront Sarah about her behavior. I was afraid of damaging our friendship or causing a rift between us. So I kept my thoughts to myself and tried to ignore the red flags that were starting to pop up.

Looking back, I can see now that I should have spoken up and addressed my concerns with Sarah earlier on. But at the time, I was too caught up in the excitement of college life and the fear of being alone to confront the reality of my situation. Little did I know that my silence would have far-reaching consequences in the months to come.

As I settled into college life with my new roommate, Sarah, I couldn't help but feel a mix of excitement and nervousness. This was my first time living away from home, and I wasn't sure what to expect.

Sarah and I got along well at first, and I was grateful to have someone to share my dorm room with. She was friendly and outgoing, and she seemed to know everyone on campus. We quickly fell into a routine of studying together in the library and hanging out with our mutual friends on the weekends.

But as the weeks went by, I started to notice some strange behavior from Sarah. She would often come home late at night, stumbling and slurring her words. I noticed that she had developed a sudden interest in partying and drinking, and she would often disappear for days at a time without any explanation.

Despite my concerns, I didn't want to confront Sarah about her behavior. I was afraid of damaging our friendship or causing a rift between us. So I kept my thoughts to myself and tried to ignore the red flags that were starting to pop up.

As time went on, Sarah's behavior became more and more erratic. She was frequently hung-over and exhausted, and she seemed to be constantly seeking out new ways to party and have fun. I couldn't help but worry about her well-being, but I didn't know how to bring up my concerns without causing conflict.

Looking back, I can see now that I should have spoken up and addressed my concerns with Sarah earlier on. But at the time, I was too caught up in the excitement of college life and the fear of being alone to confront the reality of my situation. Little did I know that my silence would have far-reaching consequences in the months to come.

Chapter Two

The Descent

As Sarah's behavior became more and more erratic, I started to worry about her well-being. I would often find empty alcohol bottles scattered around our dorm room, and Sarah would frequently come home smelling of alcohol and cigarettes. I was concerned about the amount of partying and drinking that she was doing, and I knew that it couldn't be healthy for her.

Despite my misgivings, I couldn't help but feel drawn to Sarah's reckless and carefree attitude. I had always been a bit of a goody-two-shoes, and Sarah's rebellious nature was intoxicating. I started to follow her lead, joining her on late-night partying excursions and drinking more than I ever had before.

At first, it was exciting to let go of my inhibitions and join in on the fun. But as the weeks turned into months, the partying started to take a toll on my grades and my health. I was skipping classes and failing exams, and I was constantly tired and hung-over.

Despite the negative consequences of my actions, I couldn't seem to break free from Sarah's influence. I was caught in a cycle of partying and neglecting my responsibilities, and I was too afraid to confront the reality of my situation.

Looking back, I can see now that I was in a dangerous and destructive pattern. I was corrupted by my desire to fit in and be accepted, and I was too afraid to stand up for myself and make the right decisions.

As Sarah's behavior became more and more erratic, I started to worry about her well-being. I would often find empty alcohol bottles scattered around our dorm room, and Sarah would frequently come home smelling of alcohol and cigarettes. I was concerned about the amount of partying and drinking that she was doing, and I knew that it couldn't be healthy for her.

Despite my misgivings, I couldn't help but feel drawn to Sarah's reckless and carefree attitude. I had always been a bit of a goody-two-shoes, and Sarah's rebellious nature was intoxicating. I started to follow her lead, joining her on late-night partying excursions and drinking more than I ever had before.

At first, it was exciting to let go of my inhibitions and join in on the fun. But as the weeks turned into months, the partying started to take a toll on my grades and my health. I was skipping classes and failing exams, and I was constantly tired and hung-over.

Despite the negative consequences of my actions, I couldn't seem to break free from Sarah's influence. I was caught in a cycle of partying and neglecting my responsibilities, and I was too afraid to confront the reality of my situation.

I knew that I needed to make a change, but I didn't know how to break free from Sarah's influence and take control of my own life. I was stuck in a cycle of self-destructive behavior, and I didn't know how to escape.

Looking back, I can see now that I was in a dangerous and destructive pattern. I was corrupted by my desire to fit in and be accepted, and I was too afraid to stand up for myself and make the right decisions.

Chapter Three

The Consequences

As I became more and more caught up in Sarah's destructive lifestyle, my grades began to suffer. I was skipping classes and failing exams, and I knew that I was on the brink of academic probation.

But even as the consequences of my actions became clear, I couldn't seem to break free from Sarah's influence. I was corrupted by my desire to fit in and be accepted, and I was too afraid to confront the reality of my situation.

I was constantly torn between my desire to party and have fun with Sarah, and my sense of responsibility to do well in school and achieve my goals. It was a constant battle, and I often found myself making excuses for my behavior and ignoring the warning signs.

As the weeks turned into months, I started to feel like I was drowning in a sea of negative consequences. My grades were in shambles, I was exhausted and unhealthy, and I was constantly worried about my future.

I knew that I needed to make a change, but I didn't know how to break free from Sarah's influence and take control of my own life. I was stuck in a cycle of self-destructive behavior, and I didn't know how to escape.

Looking back, I can see now that I was in a dark and dangerous place. I was completely corrupted by my desire to fit in and be accepted, and I had lost sight of my values and goals. It would take a dramatic turning point to shake me out of my complacency and set me on the path to recovery.

As I became more and more caught up in Sarah's destructive lifestyle, my grades began to suffer. I was skipping classes and failing exams, and I knew that I was on the brink of academic probation.

But even as the consequences of my actions became clear, I couldn't seem to break free from Sarah's influence. I was corrupted by my desire to fit in and be accepted, and I was too afraid to confront the reality of my situation.

I was constantly torn between my desire to party and have fun with Sarah, and my sense of responsibility to do well in school and achieve my goals. It was a constant battle, and I often found myself making excuses for my behavior and ignoring the warning signs.

As the weeks turned into months, I started to feel like I was drowning in a sea of negative consequences. My grades were in shambles, I was exhausted and unhealthy, and I was constantly worried about my future.

I knew that I needed to make a change, but I didn't know how to break free from Sarah's influence and take control of my own life. I was stuck in a cycle of self-destructive behavior, and I didn't know how to escape.

Looking back, I can see now that I was in a dark and dangerous place. I was completely corrupted by my desire to fit in and be accepted, and I had lost sight of my values and goals. It would take a dramatic turning point to shake me out of my complacency and set me on the path to recovery.

Chapter Four

The Turning Point

It wasn't until Sarah was arrested for drunk driving that I finally realized the gravity of the situation. I was shocked and terrified, and I knew that I had to make a change.

Sarah's arrest was a wake-up call for me. I realized that I couldn't continue down this path of self-destruction and neglecting my responsibilities. I knew that I needed to take control of my own life and make the right decisions, even if it meant going against the flow.

With the help of my friends and family, I was able to break free from Sarah's influence and get my life back on track. I sought counseling to deal with the emotional consequences of my experiences with Sarah, and I began working to repair the damage that I had done to my grades and my reputation.

It wasn't easy to turn my life around, but I was determined to succeed. I studied harder than ever before and made a concerted effort to surround myself with positive and supportive people.

Slowly but surely, I started to see progress. My grades began to improve, and I was able to rebuild my relationships with my friends and family. I learned the value of self-care and taking responsibility for my actions, and I committed to living a healthy and fulfilling life.

Looking back, I can see now that Sarah's arrest was the turning point that I needed to wake up and take control of my life. It was a difficult and painful experience, but it ultimately led me to a better place.

It wasn't until Sarah was arrested for drunk driving that I finally realized the gravity of the situation. I was shocked and terrified, and I knew that I had to make a change.

Sarah's arrest was a wake-up call for me. I realized that I couldn't continue down this path of self-destruction and neglecting my responsibilities. I knew that I needed to take control of my own life and make the right decisions, even if it meant going against the flow.

With the help of my friends and family, I was able to break free from Sarah's influence and get my life back on track. I sought counseling to deal with the emotional consequences of my experiences with Sarah, and I began working to repair the damage that I had done to my grades and my reputation.

It wasn't easy to turn my life around, but I was determined to succeed. I studied harder than ever before and made a concerted effort to surround myself with positive and supportive people.

Slowly but surely, I started to see progress. My grades began to improve, and I was able to rebuild my relationships with my friends and family. I learned the value of self-care and taking responsibility for my actions, and I committed to living a healthy and fulfilling life.

Looking back, I can see now that Sarah's arrest was the turning point that I needed to wake up and take control of my life. It was a difficult and painful experience, but it ultimately led me to a better place.

Chapter Five

The Lessons

Looking back, I can see now how easily I was swayed by Sarah's negative influence. I learned the hard way that it's important to stand up for what you believe in and to surround yourself with positive and supportive people.

I also learned the value of self-care and taking responsibility for my actions. It's not always easy to do the right thing, but it's always worth it in the end.

Through my experiences with Sarah, I learned that it's possible to overcome even the most difficult challenges and come out stronger on the other side. I learned that it's never too late to make a change and turn your life around, as long as you have the courage and determination to do so.

I also learned the importance of communication and honesty in relationships. I realized that it's better to be upfront and honest about your concerns and feelings, rather than keeping them bottled up inside.

Overall, my experiences with Sarah were valuable lessons in resilience and self-growth. I learned that it's never too late to make a change and turn your life around, as long as you have the courage and determination to do so. And for that, I am forever grateful.

In addition to the lessons mentioned above, I also learned the importance of setting boundaries and standing up for myself. I realized that it's okay to say no and to prioritize my well-being and values, even if it means going against the crowd.

I also learned the importance of seeking help when needed. I realized that it's okay to ask for support and to seek out resources and professionals who can help guide you through difficult times.

Finally, I learned the value of forgiveness and letting go. I realized that it's important to move on from negative experiences and to focus on the present and the future, rather than dwelling on the past.

Overall, my experiences with Sarah taught me many valuable lessons that have stayed with me to this day. I am grateful for the opportunity to learn and grow from these challenges, and I hope that my story can serve as a cautionary tale for others who may be facing similar struggles.

Looking back, I can see now how easily I was swayed by Sarah's negative influence. I learned the hard way that it's important to stand up for what you believe in and to surround yourself with positive and supportive people.

I also learned the value of self-care and taking responsibility for my actions. It's not always easy to do the right thing, but it's always worth it in the end.

Through my experiences with Sarah, I learned that it's possible to overcome even the most difficult challenges and come out stronger on the other side. I learned that it's never too late to make a change and turn your life around, as long as you have the courage and determination to do so.

I also learned the importance of communication and honesty in relationships. I realized that it's better to be upfront and honest about your concerns and feelings, rather than keeping them bottled up inside.

Overall, my experiences with Sarah were valuable lessons in resilience and self-growth. I learned that it's never too late to make a change and turn your life around, as long as you have the courage and determination to do so. And for that, I am forever grateful.

In addition to these lessons, I also learned the importance of setting boundaries and standing up for myself. I realized that it's okay to say no and to prioritize my well-being and values, even if it means going against the crowd.

I also learned the importance of seeking help when needed. I realized that it's okay to ask for support and to seek out resources and professionals who can help guide you through difficult times.

Finally, I learned the value of forgiveness and letting go. I realized that it's important to move on from negative experiences and to focus on the present and the future, rather than dwelling on the past.

Overall, my experiences with Sarah taught me many valuable lessons that have stayed with me to this day. I am grateful for the opportunity to learn and grow.

www.ingramcontent.com/pod-product-compliance
Lightning Source LLC
LaVergne TN
LVHW020535160826
845677LV00015B/4074
* 9 7 9 8 3 7 1 2 2 8 7 6 5 *